Confucius for Today

By the same authors

Erotic Wit

Don't Do It If You Can't Keep It Up

Confucius for Today

A Century of Chinese Proverbs

Gerd de Ley & David Potter

ROBERT HALE · LONDON

Selection © Gerd de Ley and David Potter 2008
English translations © David Potter 2008
First published in Great Britain 2008

ISBN 978-0-7090-8550-8

Robert Hale Limited
Clerkenwell House
Clerkenwell Green
London EC1R 0HT

www.halebooks.com

A catalogue record for this book is available from the British Library

2 4 6 8 10 9 7 5 3 1

Printed in Great Britain by
Biddles Limited, King's Lynn, Norfolk

Introduction

We have devoted a significant part of our lives to the building of a unique collection of wit, wisdom and philosophy in the form of quotations, aphorisms and, not least of all, proverbs. Our search has exposed us to many nationalities, languages and cultures and the resulting eclectic mix has given us a penetrating insight into civilizations old and new.

Our mission has been to amass a complete (or as complete as possible) international collection and translate them into a common language – English. Those that suffered a loss of subtlety in translation have been omitted.

Proverbs really know no boundaries; they are truly universal and although this selection is specifically of Chinese proverbs, they have, in fact, found their way over the centuries into all the important cultures of the world. It is their intrinsic wisdom and truth that make them eternally relevant.

Amongst the wide variety of material gathered, perhaps the most satisfying and indeed edifying experiences came from our Chinese research. Coming face to face with the monumental wisdom of the legendary Master Kung (better known by his Latinized name of Confucius) and others, has been an experience that was revealing and at the same time very humbling. The Master's influence is to be found in the greater part of all proverbs that emanate from China.

Confucius encourages in his followers a careful study of the outside world, and a process of deep thought through which to consider and judge their observations. His ideal was to achieve human perfection and he wanted his followers to develop the facility to judge matters skilfully rather than simply to learn a set of rules and live by them.

It is our sincere hope that a perusal of these pages will help the reader embrace a wider perspective of life and see things in a slightly different light. If we can absorb just a little of the profound wisdom of the Orient we will, indeed, be better equipped to interpret life around us.

Confucius's Golden Rule was 'Never impose upon others what you would not choose for yourself'. We happily impose this collection on our esteemed reader.

Gerd de Ley and David Potter

About Proverbs

A proverb is one man's wit and all men's wisdom.
John Russell

The wisdom of the wise and the experience of the ages is preserved into perpetuity by a nation's proverbs, fables, folk sayings and quotations.
William Feather

Books, like proverbs, receive their chief value from the stamp and esteem of ages through which they have passed.
William Temple

Proverbs are always platitudes until you have personally experienced the truth of them.
Aldous Huxley

Nothing ever becomes real till it is experienced – even a proverb is no proverb to you till your life has illustrated it.
John Keats

Good popular proverbs are made from ewe's milk.
Ramon Gomez de La Serna, Aphorisms, 1989

As conversation stoppers, proverbs are ideal. They seem to contain meaning, but nobody can be quite sure what it is.
Oliver Pritchett

Wise men make proverbs, but fools repeat them.
Samuel Palmer

Music-hall songs provide the dull with wit, just as proverbs provide them with wisdom.
W. Somerset Maugham

There is more in a proverb than just the words.
Frans Hiddema, Met zuinigheid en vlijt, 1992

Proverbs are short sayings made out of long experience.
Zora Neale Hurston, Moses, Man of the Mountain, 1939

Proverbs are the primers we inherit from the past.
Leo Rosen, Carnival of Wit, 1996

Chinese proverb: refined wisdom, packed in a banal one-liner.
Guido van Heulendonk, Paarden zijn ook varkens, 1995

Confucius may indeed be said to have anticipated the apothegm.
Herbert Allen Gilles, History of Chinese Literature

A country can be judged by the quality of its proverbs.
German proverb

He who wants to fool a Chinese has to rise four thousand years earlier.
Jan Wolkers

The Confucian Analects are endlessly reinterpreted: the sage must have turned over in his grave several times over because of the liberties taken in his name.
Chong Seck Chim, 'Old news and views recycled', The New Straits Times, 16 February 2000

If you have nothing wise to say, quote an ancient Chinese proverb.
Chinese proverb

ACHIEVEMENT

A great achievement has always ended with a great failure.

It is easy to take a light carriage on a familiar road.

It is easy to keep the castle that was never besieged.

It is difficult to catch a black cat in a dark room, especially when it is not there.

In the Universe the difficult things are done as if they were easy.

A cloth is not woven with one thread only.

It is not the destination that is important, but the journey there.

To have saved one human life is worth more than to build a pagoda with seven storeys.

By bending one yard, it will straighten into eight yards.

The harvest of a whole year depends on what you sow in the springtime.

Out of a tangled ball one has to draw a silk thread.

People remember a person by his accomplishments.

One bamboo cane does not make a raft.

A single fibre does not make a thread.

ACTION

You can't fill your belly painting pictures of bread.

It is better to light a candle than to curse the darkness.

The person who says it cannot be done should not interrupt the person doing it.

You'll never plough a field by turning it over in your mind.

Active people never have louse bites.

The hinge of a door is never crowded with insects.

ADVICE

Good advice is beyond price.

AMBASSADORS

An ambassador bears no blame.

A good intermediary must always be able to lie a little.

ANGER

Anger is always more harmful than the insult that caused it.

APPEARANCE

A buckle is a great addition to an old shoe.

Many a good face is under a ragged hat.

Abroad we judge the dress; at home we judge the man.

Long hair, short ideas.

People are suspicious of the man with a red nose – even if he doesn't drink at all.

Not every bald head belongs to a monk.

Big ships often sail on big debts.

Poverty and ugliness are difficult to hide.

Someone's shadow grows bigger when he is admired by the moonlight.

When you are well dressed, you don't mind if your shadow is behind you.

Beautiful flowers are ashamed when they are stuck in an old woman's hair.

Tiger, leopard, dog and sheep. They all look the same without their hair.

Your ten fingers always fold inwards.

APPEASEMENT

You do not satisfy a camel by giving him a little porridge on a spoon.

ARGUMENT

He who defines the terms wins the argument.

Insults often cover up a weak case.

ARTISTRY

A picture is a voiceless poem; a poem is a vocal picture.

ASPIRATION

He who stands on his toes will not stand upright for long.

Mountain man of the plains, why do you climb the mountain?

If you do not go up the hill you cannot see the plain.

If you want to see farther, you have to go higher.

B

BAD LUCK

Misfortune only comes in when the door is open.

BEAUTY

Beauty without virtue is like a flower with no fragrance.

Beauty is thirty per cent natural and seventy per cent make-up.

A person is three parts real and seven parts artificial – beauty needs some help.

Better a diamond with a flaw than a pebble without.

BENEVOLENCE

Benevolence is a house full of peace.

Benevolence brings honour; cruelty, disgrace.

The benevolent see benevolence, and the wise see wisdom.

BEWARE

Beware of him who has honey on his tongue and a sword around his belly.

There's always an ear on the other side of the wall, and there's bound to be someone outside the window.

When the rabbit is dead, the hunting-dog is next on the menu.

A rat who gnaws at a cat's tail invites destruction.

However strong you are, there is always someone stronger.

A weasel comes to say "Happy New Year" to the chickens.

The rose has thorns only for those who want to pick it.

BITTERNESS

Bitterness is lurking behind each joy.

The sea of bitterness has no bounds – repent and the shore is near.

Eat the wind and swallow the bitterness.

BOASTING

The boaster is like a tiger with a paper head.

Never boast – you might meet someone who knew you as a child.

A good drum does not have to be beaten hard.

Exaggeration is to paint a snake and add legs.

Stop boasting about your knowledge and you will have fewer sorrows.

It is a disgrace for a gentleman's words to be greater than his deeds.

Don't let your tongue or your paintbrush wag your tail when you are making up an inventory.

BOOKS

Every book must be chewed to get out its juice.

Copy three times a medicine-book and you are ill for the rest of your life.

Gold can be priced, but books cannot.

A book, tight shut, is but a block of paper.

You cannot open a book without learning something.

A book is like a garden carried in the pocket.

Unploughed fields make hollow bellies; unread books make hollow minds.

A dictionary can only be read when it is printed.

BRIBERY

Every brave man can lose his courage for one piece of gold.

BUSINESS

When China sneezes, Hong Kong catches pneumonia.

Credit chases customers away.

When the deal is done, discuss it no more; it is difficult to collect dispersed water.

If you don't speculate, you can't accumulate.

BUSINESSMEN

A slightly skilful businessman can register a firm in Hong Kong in the morning, open a bank account at noon and note down his first profits in the evening.

He who does not know what to do in his spare time is not a businessman.

When you go to buy, don't show your silver. From Nanking to Peking the buyers are never as smart as the sellers.

If there are many buyers in the market, the merchant doesn't wash his turnips.

He who is not eager to be paid in cash is not a businessman.

He who has never been cheated, cannot be a good business-man.

Two of a trade can never agree.

An innkeeper never worries if your appetite is big.

Pirates that attack each other seldom do good business.

He who opens a restaurant, does not bother about the great gluttony of his guests.

No melon-pedlar cries, 'Bitter melons'; no wine-dealer says, 'Sour wine'.

CATS

All cats love fish but fear to wet their paws.

CHARACTER

Adversity is a mirror that shows the real character of a man.

Can the leopard change his spots?

An ape is an ape, a varlet is a varlet.

All asses wag their ears.

He who lightly assents will seldom keep his word.

Birth is much, but breeding is more.

While the boy is small, you can see the man.

Calamity is man's true touchstone.

True character is revealed in moments of extreme anger.

If you want to know someone's character, look at the friends he keeps.

If there is beauty in character, there will be harmony in the home. If there is harmony in the home, there will be order in the nation. If there is order in the nation, there will be peace in the world.

You may change the clothes, you cannot change the man.

The last to board is the first to debark.

A whitewashed crow will not remain white for long.

There are misers who become wasteful, but never a waster became a miser.

People who easily say "yes", are seldom faithful.

The well-bred are dignified but not pompous; the ill-bred are pompous but not dignified.

Who does not trust enough will not be trusted.

You can learn more about a person in one hour of play than you can in one year of work.

A man who is inferior and is ashamed of it proves that he really is inferior.

Some wolves try to be tigers.

The tranquil is the ruler of the hasty.

Those without talents are poor. Those without ambition are weak.

When a person grows to like himself, he becomes more tolerant of others.

A person is only as big as the things that make him angry.

The former nun is more poisonous than a snake.

The daughter of a crab does not give birth to a bird.

A man can never be perfect in a hundred years; but he may become corrupt in less than a day.

A good calculator does not need artificial aids.

A courageous foe is better than a cowardly friend.

CHARITY

Alms given openly will be rewarded in secret.

Give a beggar a bed and he'll repay you with a louse.

Charity is not a bone you throw to a dog, but a bone you share with a dog.

He who waits for the surplus to give to the poor, will never give them anything.

CLEAR CONSCIENCE

If you have done no wrong, you need not fear the knock on your door at midnight.

It is better to go hungry with a pure mind than to eat well with an evil one.

A clear conscience is the best shield.

COMPASSION

Even the Goddess of Mercy sheds tears.

COMPETITION

Rivalry between scholars improves science.

COMPROMISE

Compromise is only ever a temporary success.

CONDUCT

If you are led astray by small advantages, you will never accomplish great things.

One step at a time is good walking.

He who sacrifices his conscience to ambition burns a picture to obtain the ashes.

To feed the ambition in your heart is like carrying a tiger under your arm.

He who restrains his appetite avoids debt.

Beat your drum inside the house to spare the neighbours.

Be sincere and true to your word, serious and careful in your actions; and you will get along even among barbarians.

Do not be a savage bull on the outside and a shy mouse on the inside.

Behave to everyone as if you were receiving a great guest.

It is not what beliefs we hold but what we do with those beliefs.

Blame yourself as you would blame others; excuse others as you would excuse yourself.

The first time you cheat me, be ashamed. The second time it is I who must be ashamed.

The surest way to get cheated is to believe you are smarter than the others.

The wrath of the mob is difficult to oppose.

The true gentleman does not preach what he practises till he has practised what he preaches.

Practising science and not loving men is like lighting a torch and closing your eyes.

Do not do all you can, do not spend all that you have, do not believe all that you hear, and do not tell all that you know.

Don't do it on a rainy day if you have a chance to finish on a sunny day.

Doing nothing is better than being busy doing nothing.

Large demands on oneself and little demands on others keep resentment at bay.

He who plays the donkey must not be surprised that he gets everyone on his back.

If you don't want anyone to know it, don't do it.

He who protects the qualities of others, also protects his own.

If you cannot be a shining star in the sky then be a lantern in your house.

If you cannot pay with your purse, pay with your hide.

Quietude is superior to activity.

It is hard to be right all the time, but it is easy to be wrong sometimes.

CONSEQUENCES

In nature there are neither rewards nor punishments; there are consequences.

The collapse of a dam can begin with just ant holes.

Hasty climbers have sudden falls.

If you ask for directions rudely, you may end up twenty miles from your destination.

The court official in one life has seven rebirths as a beggar.

The lotus springs from the mud.

Back to the draught is face to the grave.

Pride goes before and shame follows after.

You plant wheat, you get wheat; you plant beans, you get beans.

He who delouses other people is bitten by their fleas.

When the nest is overturned, all eggs will be broken.

The depth of the foundation determines the height of the wall.

Suspicion and guilt will make you two-faced.

He who cheats the earth will be cheated by the earth.

It cannot rain at your neighbour's place without you getting your feet wet.

Indulgences have more victims than swords.

If you behave like a machine you will have the heart of a machine.

Extreme heat produces wind.

He who has his legs spread out won't be able to march forward.

CONSIDERATION

Beat your drum inside the house to spare the neighbours.

CO-OPERATION

Behind an able man there are always other able men.

Generous souls consult each other; common people ignore advice.

What is good for the beehive is also good for the bee.

Everyone speaks well of the bridge that carries him over.

If cooks quarrel, the roast burns.

If you have enough people, you can move the palace across the river.

You can't clap with one hand.

Some roads aren't meant to be travelled alone.

COUNT YOUR BLESSINGS

Do not count the things you have lost, but the things you still have.

I was angered, for I had no shoes. Then I met a man who had no feet.

He who forgets blessings remembers insults.

COURAGE

The brave person regards dying as going home.

Better face a hazard once than always be in fear.

COWARDS

Only a coward knows what his duty is without doing it.

Those who bully the weak are cowards before the strong.

Cowards have dreams, brave people have visions.

CRIME

Every crime will tell its tale upon the day of judgment.

The best way to keep a crime a secret is not to commit it.

Rice obtained by crookedness will not boil up into good food.

One who is by nature daring and is suffering from poverty will not be lawful.

Ill-gotten gains are like snow that is sprinkled with hot water.

Negligence is the stepsister of theft.

CUSTOMS

Every hundred miles you will find different customs.

Those whose ways are different can't lay plans for one another.

Follow the local custom when you go to a foreign place.

D

DEATH

At birth we bring nothing, at death we take away nothing.

Look upon death as a going home.

Even he who has accumulated ten thousand taels of silver cannot take with him at death half a copper cash.

To die is to stop living but to stop living is something entirely different from dying.

It's better to die two years early than to live one year too long.

Get the coffin ready and the man won't die.

Of all the tools of death, desire has killed the most.

Earth will lend a grave.

Better a glorious death than a shameful life.

DEBT

Being in debt to yourself is better than being in debt to others.

The lender stands upright but he who borrows is on his knees.

DECEPTION

It is easy to evade the lance, but not the hidden sword.

DESIRE

Want a thing long enough, and you don't.

DEVIL

Talk of the devil and you'll hear the flutter of his wings.

The devil never grants long leases.

The sick devil would like to be a monk.

DISAPPOINTMENT

Great cry and little wool, as the fellow said when he sheared his pigs.

Do not try to borrow combs from shaven monks.

DISASTER

A project that you built for a long time can be destroyed in one careless moment.

Two leaps per chasm is fatal.

To complete a thing, a hundred years is not sufficient; to destroy it, one day is more than enough.

Apart from dying there are no disasters.

DISCIPLINE

To caress the same hand that administers discipline won't work for very long.

Discipline springs from love.

DISCRETION

To be discreet is far more difficult than to be eloquent.

A young man should have ears, but no mouth.

A man of high principles is someone who can watch a chess game without passing comment.

DISCRIMINATION

Better to eat a single good pear than a basket of rotten ones.

DOCTORS

It is no time to go for the doctor when the patient is dead.

No man is a good doctor who has never been sick himself.

The able doctor acts before sickness comes.

The doctor who rides in a chair will not visit the house of the poor.

Before you tell the 'truth' to the patient, be sure you know the 'truth' and that the patient wants to hear it.

DOGS

Dogs have so many friends because they wag their tails, not their tongues.

The dog will not howl if you beat him with a bone.

From the lowly perspective of a dog's eyes, everyone looks short.

Even dogs get tired of hearing the same praise over and over again.

Before you beat the dog, find out the name of his master.

DREAMS

Be careful of your dreams, they may come true.

Do not have a dream before the yellow rice is cooked.

DRINK

Of all meat in the world, drink goes down the best.

DRUNKARDS

Drunkards talk to the gods.

EARTHLY POWER

Though the emperor be rich, he cannot buy one extra year.

Emperor Ts'ong-tchen lived for eight hundred and eighty years but still not long enough to see black coal turned white.

The emperor in the capital never feels better than when those in the provinces think he is ill.

The swing of a sword can't cut the mist from the sky.

EDUCATION

Give a man a fish and you feed him for a day. Teach a man to fish and you feed him for a lifetime.

Education that only entered your eyes and your ears is like a meal you ate in your dream.

If you plan for a year, plant rice. If you plan for ten years, plant trees. If you plan for one hundred years, educate your children.

If you give a student one corner of a subject and he can't find the other three, the lesson is not worth teaching.

Nothing of what can be taught is worth learning.

A teacher is someone who ploughs with his tongue to fill his little bowl with rice.

He who teaches me for one day is my father for life.

Teachers open the door, but you must enter by yourself.

Jade stone is useless before it is processed; a man is good for nothing until he is educated.

Teach your descendants the two proper roads – literature and farming.

He who flatters me is my enemy; he who blames me is my teacher.

ENDEAVOUR

Nothing ventured, nothing gained.

To perfect diligence nothing is difficult.

The hardest step is over the threshold.

END OF THE WORLD

The end of the day is near when small men make long shadows.

A thousand pounds and a bottle of hay are all one at Doomsday.

Even oceans may at last run dry.

ENEMIES

Better an open enemy than a false friend.

When you go to dig a grave for your enemy – dig two.

He who cannot agree with his enemies is controlled by them.

Predestined enemies will always meet in a narrow alleyway.

If your enemy wrongs you, buy each of his children a drum.

ENVY

The torment of envy is like a grain of sand in the eye.

Envy shoots at others and wounds itself.

ETERNITY

The beginning and the end reach out their hands to each other.

Being and non-being produce each other.

A very large square has no visible corners.

The name that can be named is not the eternal name.

EVIL

Evil deeds done in secret are seen by the spirits as a flash of fire.

To repay evil with goods is like pouring hot water on snow.

Evil was born in someone else's underpants.

EXAMINATIONS

Examinations are a deadly struggle in the thorny enclosure.

EXCESS

Some use a cannon to shoot a sparrow.

He who has lavish desires will spend extravagantly.

EXPERIENCE

An old broom knows the dirty corners best.

Experience is a comb which nature gives us when we are bald.

If you have never been fooled, you'll never become an expert.

A fall in the pit, a gain in your wit.

Hire a young roof worker, but consult an old doctor.

If you wish to succeed, consult three old people.

Jade and men, both are sharpened by bitter tools.

If you stay long enough in one place the whole world passes you by.

You do not have to leave your house in order to discover the world.

A strong steed cannot be raised in the yard.

The older the fiddle the sweeter the tune.

To the sophisticated person, there's nothing new under the sun.

It is difficult for a snake to go back to hell once he has tasted heaven.

When one is past thirty one can about half comprehend the weather.

I do and I understand; I hear and I forget; I see and I remember.

An ounce of practice is worth a pound of theory.

You cannot appreciate the weight until you shoulder the load.

Vinegar grows more pungent with age.

FAILURE

It is not a failure to be down, but it is to stay down.

If you fall on your nose, at least you were going forward.

When the flight is not high the fall is not heavy.

When a centipede dies on the wall, the wall does not fall down.

Last night I made a thousand plans, but this morning I went my old way.

A defeat becomes a bitter drink when one decides to swallow it.

Going too far is as wrong as falling short.

It is not the failure of others to appreciate your abilities which should trouble you, but rather their failure to appreciate theirs.

FAME

Fame is empty.

The man who wakes up and find himself famous hasn't been asleep.

FAMILY

Every family has a book that is read with shame.

There is a black sow in every household.

One family builds a wall, two families enjoy it.

Man is the head of the family, woman the neck that turns the head.

Govern a family as you would cook a small fish – very gently.

It is easy to govern a kingdom but difficult to rule one's family.

When the man stays potent, the family is happy.

Ancestors

To forget one's ancestors is to be a brook without a source, a tree without a root.

Brothers

Brothers are like hands and feet.

Even the worst brother is still a brother; the best spouse is not even a blood relative.

Brothers may have a private feud.

Children

Even if a woman gives birth to nine children, each child is different.

Beat your child once a day.

A child's life is like a piece of paper on which every passer-by leaves a mark.

Good offspring are better than material wealth.

Daughters

The families of elegant daughters are the worst thieves.

An unmarried daughter is like a sack of rice on which tax is not yet paid.

No wise man takes responsibility for an 18-year-old daughter.

Daughters-in-law

When there are too many daughters-in-law; the kettle never gets cleaned.

When a family runs into trouble, the oldest daughter-in-law grows a beard.

Fathers

Nobody mourns for the father of everybody.

Fathers and sons

The father who does not teach his son his duties is equally guilty with the son who neglects them.

The son must bury his father, the father must marry his son.

Grandfathers

Grandfather built the street in which father drives his car.

Grandfather is the wisest person in the house but few of the household listen.

Grandparents

The house with an old grandparent harbours a jewel.

Husbands

A man thinks that he knows it all, but his wife knows better.

Mothers

Even the meanest wolf will not devour its own mother.

You can abandon your father, even if he is a judge, but you can't abandon your mother, even if she is a beggar.

Call her 'mother' once and she will become your mother forever.

Mothers-in-law

If you want to play, go to your grandmother's house; if you are looking for trouble, go to your mother-in-law's.

Mothers-in-law are always gossiping, so daughters-in-law should be hard of hearing.

If you want a favour from your husband's mother, flatter first her youngest sister.

Parents

Parents cherish their youngest son; grandparents their oldest grandson.

Parents who are afraid to put their feet down usually have children who step on their toes.

There are no filial children at the bedside of chronically ill parents.

Sons

A son that makes his mother weep is the only one that can dry her tears.

You are more intimate with your grandson than with your son.

Brainless sons boast of their ancestors.

Widows

A widow is a boat without a rudder.

At the widow's gate many a scandal will occur.

Only a widow knows the widow's grief.

The young girl receives a husband; the widow takes one.

A maiden marries to please her parents, a widow to please herself.

A widow's tears will flow; with widowers lice will grow.

Wives

Marry your wife for her virtues; take a concubine for her beauty.

It is easier to rule a country than to rule your wife.

If she does not cry on her wedding day, she won't be happy.

She who is the wife of one man cannot eat the rice of two.

It takes a hundred soldiers to make a camp, but only one wife to make a home.

Do not curse your wife after sundown, unless you want to sleep alone.

Beat your wife as much as you want, as long as the stick is not longer than your thumb.

Good wives have bad husbands and good husbands have bad wives.

Good wife, carefree life.

Men love themselves and other people's wives.

A man thinks that he knows it all, but his wife knows better.

Don't argue with your wife at night, or you will end up sleeping alone the next several nights.

A man does not leave his wife, the scales do not leave the weights.

If you don't beat your wife every three days, she'll start tearing up roof tiles.

Teach your son in the front garden and your wife on the pillow.

The young wife is treated like sandals of straw, the older wife like a grandmother.

There is no end to the resistance of a virgin or the wrath of your wife.

There's no end either to a virgin's resistance or to a wife's resentment.

The wife who deceives her husband makes her lover swear never to be unfaithful to her.

Wives and eunuchs can be neither taught nor led.

The ugly housewife is a treasure at home.

Whoever buys a house must examine the beams; whoever wants a wife must look at her mother.

FARMERS

No matter how clever the farmer is, he will never grow sunflowers without seed.

Better dry one tear on the face of a farmer than get a hundred smiles from a minister.

The farmer hopes for rain, the walker hopes for sunshine and the gods hesitate.

Where the tiller is tireless, the land is fertile.

FATE

What you cannot avoid, welcome.

What is destined to be yours, will always come back to you.

Often one finds one's destiny just where one hides to avoid it.

When fate smiles at us, we meet friends; when fate is against us, we meet a beautiful woman.

What is fated to be yours will always return to you.

FAULTS

He who hides his faults plans to make more.

Deal with the faults of others as gently as with your own.

Think of your own faults the first part of the night when you are awake, and of the faults of others the latter part of the night when you are asleep.

FEAR

He who is afraid of nothing, is surprised by danger.

There is no greater illusion than fear.

Whoever can see through all fear will always be safe.

Once bitten by a snake, he is scared all his life at the mere sight of a rope.

Honour and shame give birth to the same fear.

FIRE

You can cover up fire, but you cannot hide smoke.

Don't open your clothes to embrace a fire.

FISH

If you are not a fish, how can you know if the fish are happy?

A dried fish cannot be used as a cat's pillow.

In a pool without fish the shrimps are highly praised.

The fish sees the bait but not the hook.

Those who don't get their feet wet don't catch fish.

All rotten fish tastes the same.

FOLLY

The most stupid bird flies upwards.

When a finger is pointing at the moon, the fool looks at the finger.

A fool in a hurry drinks tea with a fork.

A man who knows that he is a fool is not a great fool.

He who asks a question may be a fool for five minutes; he who asks no questions stays a fool forever.

A fool is someone who wants to empty the ocean with a little spoon.

Only a fool will wait for an obedient girl.

Silly toad: planning a meal of goose!

FOOD

He who always eats the roots of a plant is capable of anything.

One cannot refuse to eat just because there is a chance of being choked.

If you want to live one more year, you will have to eat one bite less every meal.

Anything that walks, swims, crawls, or flies with its back to heaven is edible.

Even a great feast has a last course.

The delicacy of the feast is the learned guest.

Enough food and a pipeful of tobacco makes you equal to the immortals.

Healthy food cures better than medicine.

A divided orange tastes just as good.

No matter how big the world is, it is still difficult to fill one bowl with rice.

FORESIGHT

He who could foresee affairs three days in advance would be rich for a thousand years.

To know precisely when to start the ploughing is better than having the best plough.

FORETHOUGHT

Chi Wen Tzu always thought three times before taking action. Twice would have been quite enough.

Dig a ditch while the sky is clear, or you'll have a flood when it rains.

Be thrifty in winter or you'll have worries in the spring; be industrious in the summer or you'll have no harvest in the autumn.

If you are prepared for difficulties, they won't come.

Forethought is easy, repentance hard.

Use the days of plenty to think of days of nothing.

The more you sweat in peacetime, the less you bleed during war.

You must lay a foundation before you build a wall, and you must raise a chicken before you gather eggs.

Dig the well before you are thirsty.

Clumsy birds better take off a little earlier.

When you don't think far in advance, you will quickly start to go backwards.

An ounce of prevention is worth a pound of cure.

Sow early and you will reap early.

Think before you speak; but do not say everything you think.

A clever rabbit has a burrow with three holes.

Take a second look; it costs you nothing.

FOREWARNED

Forewarned is forearmed.

FORGIVENESS

Women and fools never forgive.

A fool cannot forgive; he who can forgive is not a fool.

Weaklings never forgive their enemies.

FREEDOM

If the string is long, the kite flies high.

If you let go then you have both hands free.

The best things in life are free.

FRIENDSHIP

He who abuses you to your face, can still be a friend.

The more acquaintances you have, the less you know them.

Ceremony is the smoke of friendship.

A broken relationship is hard to put back together.

When men are friendly the water is sweet.

There is a no better sale than when you give a true friend what he needs.

If you drink with a friend, a thousand cups are too few; if you argue with a man, half a sentence is too much.

Your friend has a friend; don't tell him.

A friend – one soul, two bodies.

Quarrel with a friend – and you are both wrong.

Do not remove a fly from your friend's forehead with a hatchet.

First time strangers, second time friends.

FUTURE

Coming events cast their shadows before them.

All the past died yesterday; the future is born today.

You can take precautions against the future, but not against the past.

When men speak of the future, the Gods laugh.

Don't try to make predictions – especially those concerning the future.

One generation builds the street on which the next will walk.

The past remembered is a good guide for the future.

GAMBLING

There are no winners among habitual gamblers.

He who can persuade someone not to gamble has earned money for him.

GARDENERS

He who plants a garden plants happiness.

Life begins the day you start a garden.

All gardeners know better than other gardeners.

GENERALS

A great general does not need to blow his own trumpet.

A general's triumph means ten thousand rotting bones.

When the general is strong, there are no weak soldiers.

The timid can't become generals.

GENEROSITY

If you always give, you will always have.

The scent of a rose will always stay on the hand of the giver.

GENIUS

Genius can be recognized by its childish simplicity.

Genius does what it must; talent does what it can.

To see things in the seed, that is genius.

Before the beginning of great brilliance, there must be chaos.

GHOSTS

No one is more afraid of ghosts than those who don't believe in them.

The more you are afraid of ghosts, the more ghosts you see.

GIFTS

Gifts reflect those who give them.

In the long run, whatever you're given you pay for.

The first favour is a favour, the second an obligation.

GIRLS

A girl of eighteen looks like a flower.

A girl that blushes too much, knows too much.

Do not let a girl visit her older sister's husband.

When girls plough there will be three years of drought.

GLUTTONY

Greed is always hungry.

Greedy for an extra piece of meat; you end up losing the whole sheep.

A glutton is able to take off his skull in order to stuff himself more quickly with food.

GOLD

Real gold is not afraid of the melting pot.

The gold does not belong to the miser, but the miser to the gold.

GOOD DEEDS

Good deeds stay at home, bad deeds echo a thousand miles.

GOOD LUCK

If luck is against you, even water will stick in your teeth.

Nobody will be lucky forever, just as flowers will not blossom for a hundred days.

Good luck beats early rising.

You can't stay at the top of the wheel of fortune for ever.

Fortune knocks but thrice.

Good luck seldom comes in pairs but bad things never walk alone.

GOVERNMENT

When those in authority are corrupt, everybody tends to follow suit.

Governments are gluttons for taxes; that is why the people starve.

Corporations have neither bodies to be punished nor souls to be damned.

GRATITUDE

A grateful man has no need to blush.

GREAT WALL OF CHINA

Look beneath the Great Wall, and you will see bones upon bones of dead men.

The great wall stands; the builder is gone.

GREED

The avarice of a man is like a snake trying to swallow an elephant.

Gold and silver are mingled with dirt, till avarice parted them.

HAPPINESS

To be able to curse once a day improves happiness and lengthens life.

Happiness is someone to love, something to do, and something to hope for.

Men fated to be happy need not hasten.

Make happy those who are near, and those who are far will come.

We are happy because we are not aware that we are happy.

Stolen joys are always the sweetest.

When joy is extreme it is the forerunner of grief.

HATRED

After great hatred, a little hatred is left behind.

HEALING

Nature, time and patience are the three great physicians.

HEALTH

One hundred bodies cannot make good a broken leg.

Health is not valued until illness comes.

To avoid sickness eat less; to prolong life worry less.

Open the window and improve your health.

A walk after a meal makes for a long life.

HEART

A person with a determined heart frightens problems away.

If I keep a green bough in my heart, the singing bird will come.

If the heart does not co-operate, the hands will have no skill.

There is a bottom to the Huang River, but none to the human heart.

Consult the oracles only after your heart has decided.

What the eyes do not see, the heart does not feel.

HEAVEN

Heaven is only three feet above your head.

If Heaven above lets fall a plum, open your mouth.

Heaven lent you a soul.

If Heaven creates a man, earth can find some use for him.

Better go to Heaven in rags than to Hell in embroidery.

Men's whispers sound like thunder in Heaven's ears; their secret thoughts flash like lightning before Heaven's eyes.

HELL

There are no fans in hell.

HONESTY

Honesty is the only currency with which you can pay everywhere.

Where honesty is not enough, there can be no honesty at all.

HOPE

The darkest hour is that before the dawn.

HOSPITALITY

If at home you receive no visitors, then abroad you will have no host.

HUNGER

Hungry mouths will even melt metal.

A starving man is not fussy about his food.

I

IGNORANCE

Ignorance is not the night of the mind, but a night without moon or star.

IMMORTALITY

One bite of the peach of immortality is worth more than a basket full of apricots.

IMPATIENCE

A little impatience spoils great plans.

Impatient people talk too much.

Desire to have things done quickly prevents their being done thoroughly.

IMPERFECTION

The worst cracks are to be found in the most beautiful vases.

INEXPERIENCE

New-born calves are not afraid of tigers.

INJUSTICE

It is more difficult not to complain of injustice when poor than to behave with arrogance when rich.

An injustice is nothing if you can forget it.

INSANITY

Insanity is doing the same thing in the same way and expecting a different outcome.

INSINCERITY

The bigger the compliments, the smaller the tenderness.

'No' said a hundred times is less painful than one insincere 'yes'.

INSPIRATION

Inspiration comes only after perspiration.

INTEGRITY

One body cannot perform two services.

He who has a straight body is not worried about his crooked shadow.

The true man will not compromise his principles for a meagre reward.

The scale and the measuring glass were invented because not everybody has an honest heart.

Slander cannot make a good man bad: when the flood recedes the rock is there.

Even a good horse cannot wear two saddles.

Do not stand with your right foot on one boat and your left on another.

Mud can hide a robin but it will not make him dirty.

INTELLIGENCE

Never has a man more need of his intelligence than when a fool asks him a question.

To have emotions without intelligence is a misery; to have intelligence without emotions is a barren desert.

JEALOUSY

Jealousy arises often from a narrow heart.

JUDGE

Do not trouble the judge when you are right but penniless.

Even the best judge cannot settle a domestic dispute.

JUDGEMENT

Abroad we judge the dress; at home we judge the man.

When you are involved you are bewildered; when you are not involved you see things clearly.

Those who play the game do not see as clearly as those who watch.

JUSTICE

When the prince breaks the law, he should be punished like everyone else.

Killing a bad monarch is not to be considered murder but justice.

Do not judge someone before his coffin is closed.

Though the sword of justice be sharp, it will not slay the innocent.

KINDNESS

Forget injuries, never forget kindnesses.

It is better to do a kindness near home than go far to burn incense.

KNOWLEDGE

With money you can buy a book, but not knowledge.

LAWS

Laws are useless when people behave; impracticable when they are corrupt.

The more laws made, the more criminals created.

LAWSUITS

Win your lawsuit and lose your money.

Going to law is losing a cow for the sake of a cat.

The year-long trial breeds ten years of rancour.

LAZINESS

Taking action without doing anything makes a lot of rules superfluous.

Nodding the head does not row the boat.

It takes little effort to watch a man carry a load.

A man grows most tired while standing still.

Lazy people always want to do everything at the same time.

A long tongue is a sign of a short hand.

A man must sit with his mouth open for a long time before a roast duck flies in.

LEADERS

Be gentle and you can be bold; be frugal and you can be liberal; avoid putting yourself before others and you can become a leader among men.

The most successful manager leads without dictating.

When the effective leader is finished with his work, the people say it happened naturally.

A leader is best when people hardly know he exists.

To lead the people, walk behind them.

The best tacticians are never impulsive and the best leaders are never arrogant.

One sings, all follow.

LEARNING

You have to study to learn to be good.

He who fills his head instead of his pockets, can never be robbed.

Learning is a treasure no thief can touch.

Those who do not study are only cattle dressed up in men's clothes.

Learning is weightless treasure you can always carry easily.

It is better to learn one thing thoroughly than to know ten things superficially.

LIES

Big lies are made from half truths.

The longer the explanation, the bigger the lie.

Nine out of ten matchmakers are liars.

The three times liar is never believed.

LIFE

The miracle is not to fly in the air, or to walk on the water, but to walk on the earth.

Life's journey is the reward.

Our body is the Universe in miniature.

An old bachelor compares life with a shirt button that hangs often by a thread.

All things change, and we change with them.

Shade and light are different in every valley.

For everything there is a cause.

Life begins at seventy.

Life is but a smile on the lips of death.

Life is a tragedy for those who feel and a comedy for those who think.

Life is a dream walking; death is a going home.

Life isn't measured by how many breaths we take, but by the moments that take our breath away.

LIGHT

A bright light in a dark tunnel is brighter than all the lights in a seven-storey temple.

The light of a hundred stars does not equal the light of the moon.

When the lamps in the house are lit it is like the flowering of lotus on the lake.

Ten night lights are not worth one lamp.

LIMITATIONS

Limitations are only borders we create for ourselves.

A large bull cannot pick his own lice.

No matter how big, one beam cannot support a house.

Little posts cannot support heavy weights.

LOSS

You cannot lose what you have never had.

LOVE

A couple that has one happy day together, is blessed with a hundred days of tenderness.

The love that isn't deep is quickly broken.

Being deeply loved by someone gives you strength, while loving someone deeply gives you courage.

Love has many eyes, but only looks in one direction.

When a man is crazy about a woman only she can cure him.

A great lover is not one who romances a different woman every night. A great lover is one who romances the same woman for a lifetime.

Spouses that love each other say a thousand things without speaking.

LOYALTY

Without traitors, the loyal do not stand out.

Public before private and country before family.

MARRIAGE

The perfect marriage is like the blossom of flowers by a full moon.

Keeping your chastity is not as good as marrying again.

Husband and wife in perfect concord are like the music of the harp and lute.

Dream of a funeral and you hear of a marriage.

Wedlock is a padlock.

The girl will have little fortune if she doesn't cry on her wedding ceremony.

An extravagant wedding hurts both sides of the family.

Ugly men marry pretty wives.

MEDICINE

If the medicine is bitter, it must be good.

Medicine cures the man who is fated not to die.

Laughter is the medicine to cure one hundred illnesses.

A single untried popular remedy often throws the scientific doctor into hysterics.

Adapt the remedy to the disease.

The herb that can't be got is the one that heals.

MEMORY

A good memory is not so good as a little ink.

The palest ink is better than the best memory.

Remembering is for those who have forgotten.

Shame is forgotten, debts are not.

MEN

A man who pats himself on the back risks a broken arm.

A man is like a child born at midnight; when he sees the sun, he doesn't know that yesterday ever existed.

A man is worth more than he is paid.

A man combs his hair every morning – why not his heart?

A man should have a child, plant a tree and write a book.

A man is all the more rich for giving away something he really needs.

Good men

There are two perfectly good men, one dead, and the other unborn.

Great men

The great man acts before he speaks, and afterwards speaks according to his action.

The great man is slow in his words and earnest in his conduct.

What the great man seeks is in himself. What the mean man seeks is in others.

A great man is hard on himself. A small man is hard on others.

Wise men

The wise man looks into space and he knows there are no limited dimensions.

The wise man doesn't stand beneath a collapsing wall.

Wise is he who listens to his body.

Wise people are not always learned; learned people are not always wise.

The wise man and the tortoise travel but never leave their home.

The wise man learns more from his enemies than a fool does from his friends.

The wise man, although he keeps in the background, stays ahead.

Clever men are often the servants of fools.

The sage manages affairs without action and spreads doctrines without words.

A wise man takes good advice to heart but it goes no further than the fool's ears.

The wise man puts himself last and finds himself first.

A fall will always make a wise man wiser.

A wise man who has seen everything is not the equal of one who has done one thing with his hands.

The truly wise man doesn't display his wisdom.

A single conversation across the table with a wise man is worth a month's study of books.

A wise man will not reprove a fool.

Only the very wise and the very stupid never change their minds.

The more a wise man gives to others, the more he has for himself.

A wise man adapts himself to circumstances, as water shapes itself to the vessel that contains it.

The wise man looks at all sides of a question; the petty man can only see one side.

The wise man doesn't say what he does but he never does what can't be said.

No matter how much the wise man travels, he always lives in the same place.

Wise men are never in a hurry.

MEN AND WOMEN

A man thinks he knows, but a woman knows better.

Men love their own compositions and other men's wives.

It's not the beauty of a woman that blinds the man, the man blinds himself.

In the field the good grain is the other fellow's; on the road the pretty woman is the other man's wife.

MESSENGERS

No one believes a crow bearing good news.

MISTAKES

It is a mistake to make a mistake and not correct it.

Always leave a little room for a mistake.

MOCKERY

Mockery is the flashing of slander.

MODESTY

Modesty is the companion of success.

MONEY

With money, a dragon – without it, a worm.

If two men unite, their money will buy gold.

Money, in the hands of a bachelor, is as good as gone.

If you don't spend the small money; the big money will not come.

Money allows you to speak to the gods.

Nobility is what is earned by those who have no other earnings.

Lend money to a bad debtor and he will hate you.

He who hasn't a penny, sees bargains everywhere.

With money you can buy a bed but not sleep.

A thousand taels won't purchase a laugh.

MUSIC

Music pleases the heart and warms the mind.

NEED

If you do without something for long enough, then you don't need it.

What you throw away today, you'll probably need tomorrow.

NOVELTY

New things always smell good.

OBESITY

Obesity is not the result of a single bite.

By the time that fat people get thin, the thin have been dead for ages.

OLD AGE

Do not tremble at the thought of being old and weak; tremble because your heart gets cold though you are still young.

Some people are already old when they are three.

An old man in love is like a flower in winter.

An old man has crossed more bridges than a young man has crossed streets.

Elderly people say that every new year is worse than the one before.

Though his hair is white, he is as young as ever.

OPINIONS

Opinions are like nails: the more often you hit them the deeper they penetrate.

OPPORTUNITY

Opportunity must not be lost while the gods smile.

Opportunities multiply as they are seized.

One who has time to complain has time to submit patches.

A crisis is an opportunity riding the dangerous wind.

OTHER PEOPLE

Other men are the carving knife and serving dish; we are the fish and the meat.

OVERREACTION

There are those who burn the entire wood just to chase away the wolves.

Do not burn your house to get rid of the mouse.

OWNERSHIP

He who keeps the hills, burns the wood; he who keeps the streams drinks the water.

There is no one to sweep a common hall.

PAIN

Pain is easier to endure than an itch.

PATIENCE

Patience for a while, rest for a moment, forget a mistake, take a step back, and you will see the whole picture.

Patience is wisdom in waiting.

Patience is like a tree that has bitter roots, but gives sweet fruit.

For those who can wait, time opens its doors.

Patience, and the mulberry leaf becomes a silk gown.

Do not pull the seedlings to make them grow faster.

PATRIOTISM

When a nation is filled with strife then do patriots flourish.

PEACE

Only in times of peace can a grain of sand change into a pearl.

PEACEMAKING

An answer that does not resolve a quarrel, makes a thousand new ones.

PEOPLE

All people are your relatives, therefore expect only trouble.

Some people are easy to serve but difficult to please.

Some people point at Sang and scold Huai.

PERFECTION

Flies never visit an egg that has no crack.

PERSEVERANCE

An ant may well destroy a whole dam.

Steady application makes a superior product.

Constant effort yields certain success.

Your goal is just around the corner.

Deviate an inch, lose a thousand miles.

If you get up one more time than you fall, you will make it through.

An oak is not felled at one stroke.

Enough feathers can sink a boat.

It does not matter how slowly you go so long as you do not stop.

If we don't change our direction we're likely to end up where we're headed.

If you neglect your art for one day it will neglect you for two.

Know deeply the depths and the details.

It is easier to know how to do a thing than to do it.

The itch that gives someone skill is difficult to scratch.

The first thing to do is to start and the second is to continue.

Our greatest glory is not in never failing, but in rising every time we fail.

PHILANTHROPY

Heaven and earth don't practice philanthropy.

PHILOSOPHY

Philosophy had its golden age when there were no philosophers.

With a frog in the well you don't talk about the ocean.

PHOENIX

You cannot attract a phoenix without a parasol tree.

PITY

To rely on other people's pity is as foolish as it is to expect the candle's flame to resist the wind.

Those with one eye only will take pity on the blind.

POLITENESS

When your neighbour walks through your orchard, the polite thing to do is to ignore it.

Only lambs are polite enough to suck on their knees.

Great politeness usually means 'I want something'.

If you want dinner, don't insult the cook.

He who steps aside for someone broadens the way.

A rose has no back.
(Chinese reply if you apologize for turning your back)

POLITICS

Politics makes strange bedfellows.

POSSESSIONS

A trout in the pot is better than a salmon in the sea.

Thinking that possessions will fulfil your desires is like thinking that you can extinguish a fire with a bundle of straw.

POVERTY

Better to die ten years early than live ten years poor.

A cold man can't be choosy about clothes.

The thief is no danger to the beggar.

To move into a new house means three years of poverty.

He who is without cash in his pocket might as well be buried in a rice tub with his mouth sewed up.

It is as difficult to be poor without complaining, as it is to be rich without boasting about it.

POWER

He who steals a country becomes its master.

The less power a man has, the more he likes to use it.

A wheel is made of thirty spokes, but it is turned by the axis.

PROBLEM-SOLVING

Minimise big problems by dividing them into several small ones.

Settle one difficulty, and you keep a hundred others away.

Impasse is followed by change, and change will lead to a solution.

Use one thorn to extract another.

PUNISHMENT

Disobedience is the mother of a whipped back.

The best way to avoid punishment is to fear it.

Excessive scoldings and beatings lose their intended effect.

QUARRELS

Reduce big quarrels to small ones and small ones to nothing.

R

RAIN

If rain bothers you, you can always jump into the sea.

The stronger the thunder, the weaker the rain.

The roof tiles that protect you against the rain, were made while the weather was fine.

READING

After three days without reading, talk becomes flavourless.

A day of reading is a day of gain; a day without reading is ten days of loss.

REASON

Reason goes further than the heart, but never far.

RELIGION

A Buddha made of mud, cannot save himself when crossing the river.

He who carves the Buddha never worships him.

Burn the right incense in the right temple.

The broad-minded see the truth in different religions; the narrow-minded see only the differences.

Don't burn false incense before a true god.

An image-maker never worships the Buddha.

The priest from a far-off land will read the rites better.

If you do not fear the gods, just listen to the thunder.

REMORSE

You cannot undo a stupid act by reproaching yourself.

REPUTATION

Reputation is like a cake drawn on the ground. If you're hungry, it's not much help.

Your reputation is your second life.

RESERVE

Reserve builds a fortress in the mind.

RESPECT

One looks at a worthy person as at a mountain.

In the presence of princes the cleverest jester is mute.

REUNION

Reunion after a brief separation is better than a honeymoon.

REVENGE

He who takes revenge for a small insult, will have a bigger one thrown at him.

He who seeks revenge should remember to dig two graves.

RIVERS

One hundred rivers return to the sea.

A great river is the result of many little drops.

RULERS

If the ruler sets a good example, the people will be easy to manage.

The less kings and beautiful women speak, the more they say.

When a king makes a mistake, all the people suffer.

Governors should not use water for a mirror, but the people.

If a man becomes powerful even his chicken and his dog go to heaven.

RULES FOR LIFE

Small is beautiful.

Put up or shut up.

You can't get tender shoots from a rotten bamboo stalk.

A good breakfast cannot take the place of the evening meal.

Three times an early rise makes a whole day.

To be uncertain is to be uncomfortable, but to be certain is to be ridiculous.

Don't cut off your nose to spite your face.

You cannot eat a bun from the middle.

We must always have old memories and young hopes.

Idleness breeds lust.

To stop drinking, study a drunkard when you are sober.

O eggs, never fight with stones!

Enjoy yourself. It's later than you think.

Do not play a flute before a cow.

What's the use of playing a lute to a donkey?

Don't let the falcon loose until you see the hare.

Talking doesn't get your rice cooked.

Better to drink one cup of tea in this world than to eat a plate of rice in the next.

The day of the storm is not the time for thatching.

Do not think any vice trivial, and so practise it; do not think any virtue trivial, and so neglect it.

There is no economy in going to bed early to save candles if the result is twins.

Real people know that what is far away can also be found nearby.

You must chop before you can plane, and cut before you can polish.

To be wronged is nothing unless you continue to remember it.

You can't expect both ends of a sugar cane to be equally sweet.

No needle is sharp at both ends.

You cannot build a wall with ashes.

He who treads softly goes far.

Never do anything standing that you can do sitting, or anything sitting that you can do lying down.

He who stands still in the mud sticks in it.

The careful foot can walk anywhere.

Use the days of plenty to think of days of nothing.

Be sincere and true to your word, serious and careful in your actions; and you will get along even among barbarians.

Never eat in a restaurant where the chef is thin.

Do not dress in clothes made of leaves when going to put out a fire.

He who hurries cannot walk with dignity.

If you suspect a man, don't employ him, and if you employ him, don't suspect him.

There are three kinds of person that you must not challenge: civil servants, customers and widows.

He who allows himself to be given away is not worth being accepted again.

Don't promise something when you are full of joy; don't answer letters when you are full of anger.

Better to depart on good terms than to arrive on good terms.

Cross the road for only four things: a fallen tree, your boss, concubines who whisper to each other unanimously and a goat with a leopard's tail.

What is in the marrow is hard to take out of the bone.

The little pot is soonest hot.

What is not urgent must be done quickly in order to take care of the urgent things calmly.

Do not tear down the east wall to repair the west.

Warmth for everyone, cold for yourself.

Be sceptical; long garments can also hide big feet.

On one day in the week, if possible, neither read nor write poetry.

To ask is not a crime. To be rejected is not a calamity.

Do not take the seeds and throw away the melon.

Large roosters don't eat fine rice.

You can't beat oil out of chaff.

If you beat spice it will smell the sweeter.

That which is quickly acquired is easily lost.

An easy promise is hard to keep.

RUMOURS

A false report rides post haste.

When gossip is on the lips of thousands it becomes an irrefutable fact.

'I heard' is not as good as 'I saw'.

Don't listen to what they say. Go see.

S

SECRETS

The best kept secrets are those you keep for yourself.

SELF-CONTROL

If you can command yourself, you can command the world.

You need true heroism to conquer yourself.

He who beats himself is the strongest knight.

Control your emotion or it will control you.

He who is always mild-mannered is invincible.

SELF-CRITICISM

You must despise yourself before the others do.

A man must insult himself before others will.

SELF-DECEPTION

A fly before his own eye is bigger than an elephant in the next field.

People fool themselves. They pray for a long life but fear old age.

The snake says: 'The road is winding, not I.'

SELF-DOUBT

He who thinks too much about every step he takes, will stay on one leg all his life.

SELF-IMPROVEMENT

When you meet someone better than yourself, turn your thoughts to becoming his equal.

SELFISHNESS

He who goes his own way does not deserve to be received.

SELF-KNOWLEDGE

Do not be concerned at other men's not knowing you; be concerned at your own want of ability.

He who knows others is learned, and he who knows himself is wise.

Mistrust yourself before others do.

Know thyself to know others, for heart beats like heart.

Who is not satisfied with himself will grow; who is not sure of his own correctness will learn many things.

He who wants to know himself should offend two or three of his neighbours.

When you lose, don't lose the lesson.

Before you prepare to improve the world, look around your own house three times.

SELF-PRAISE

He who praises himself, stinks.

SELF-PRESERVATION

The most important kind of protection is that of oneself.

You must have crossed the river before you may tell the crocodile he has bad breath.

A blind man can see his mouth.

The blind are quick at hearing; the deaf are quick at sight.

Never lift up a stone to let it fall on your own foot.

When you want to test the depths of a stream, don't use both feet.

Herons do not eat herons' flesh.

The one-legged never stumble.

Don't look back when you are walking along the edge of a wall.

If you are standing on the edge of an abyss, don't step back.

SELF-RELIANCE

The best place to find helping hands is at the end of your own arms.

You've got to do your own growing, no matter how tall your grandfather is.

A sparrow may be small but it has everything it needs.

SERENDIPITY

An accidental meeting is more pleasant than a planned one.

SERVANTS

Believe your servants but do not listen to them.

Do not employ handsome servants.

SEX

One cannot manage too many affairs: like pumpkins in the water, one pops up while you try to hold down the other.

Good behaviour is a virtue for the man – bad behaviour is the virtue of a woman.

The gate that gave life to you, can also be the gate that leads to your death.

The wrinkle between her legs is the smile of life.

With money you can buy sex but not love.

Seldom does anyone prefer virtue to sexual delight.

Kissing is like drinking salted water: you drink, and your thirst increases.

Prostitutes are willows along the road, flowers on a wall.

Passion too deep seems like none.

No sex till a hundred days after giving birth for those who want to live long and happily with their wives.

SHOPKEEPERS

He who cannot laugh should not open a shop.

SICKNESS

When you are ill for long enough, you become a skilled physician.

SILENCE

Silence is a true friend who never betrays.

The stars make no noise.

A hamster is like a human being: only quiet when it is underground.

SIN

All sins cast long shadows.

He who swims in sin shall sink in sorrow.

SINGLE-MINDEDNESS

He who walks on two roads at the same time, arrives nowhere.

Even a skilled hand can't sew two needles at the same time.

If you are hunting for a red deer then ignore the hares.

SLEEP

The loss of one night's sleep is followed by ten days of inconvenience.

He who cannot sleep says his bed was badly made.

SMILES

Smile three times a day and you won't need any medicine.

Some smiles hide a knife.

He who smiles in all directions only gets wrinkles in his face.

When the mouth smiles, the heart smiles.

If you have nothing else to offer me – offer me your smile.

SOLITUDE

Is there, in this sea of a world of ours, a wave that is quite alone?

You can only enjoy solitude when you are at peace with yourself.

He who keeps his door closed lives in the middle of a desert.

SONGBIRD

A bird does not sing because he has the answer to something, he sings because he has a song.

A dead songbird gives us a sad meal.

SORROW

One day of sorrow lasts longer than a month full of joy.

You cannot prevent the birds of sorrow from flying over your head, but you can prevent them from building nests in your hair.

Two barrels of tears will not heal a bruise.

SPIRITUAL LIFE

A butcher becomes a Buddha the moment he drops his cleaver.

The spirit goes on foot.

The spirit never perishes, only the body decays.

It is better to offer your prayers to the spirits than to man.

Without the aid of the divine, man cannot walk even an inch.

Music in the soul can be heard by the universe.

SPRING

Spring is sooner recognized by plants than by men.

STEALING

It is easier to go and steal for a thousand days than to protect your house against thieves for a thousand days.

Steal a bell with one's ears covered.

It is not easy to steal where the landlord is a thief.

He who steals a belt, pays for it with his life.

Not collecting treasures prevents stealing.

STORYTELLER

A good storyteller must be able to lie a little.

STUPIDITY

Rascality has limits; stupidity has not.

The more stupid, the happier.

SUCCESS

Mutual assistance makes mutual success.

Success is three parts genius and seven parts hard work.

The key to success isn't much good until one discovers the right lock to put it in.

When a man gets to the top, his friends and relatives accompany him.

You cannot propel yourself forward by patting yourself on the back.

No sweet without sweat.

Those who have not tasted the bitterest of life's bitters can never appreciate the sweetest of life's sweets.

In shallow waters, shrimps make fools of dragons.

The silent duck gets the worm.

SUN

It is not necessary to light a candle to the sun.

The sun has risen twice today.
  Chinese saying on meeting you unexpectedly

You can't cut off the sunlight with one hand.

SURVIVAL

Of all the thirty-six alternatives, running away is best.

He that fights and runs away may live to fight another day.

Better a live beggar than a dead king.

After being struck on the head by an axe it is a positive pleasure to be beaten about the body with a wooden club.

It is better to save your innocence at the expense of your honour than your country at the expense of your life.

A reed before the wind lives on, while mighty oaks do fall.

A scholar's ink lasts longer than a martyr's blood.

τ

TACT

To make good conversation there are a thousand subjects, but there are still those who cannot meet a cripple without talking about feet.

A courteous man does not even step on the shadow of his fellow man.

When with dwarfs, do not talk about pygmies.

TALK

The tongue is like a sharp knife: it kills without drawing blood.

Where the tongue slips, it speaks the truth.

Better the foot slip than the tongue trip.

Don't talk unless you can improve the silence.

Talking without thinking is shooting without aiming.

Four horses cannot overtake the tongue.

TEA

If you want good tea, then first look for good water.

Better to drink the weak tea of a friend than the sweet wine of an enemy.

A girl can't drink tea from two families.

Tea tempers the spirit, harmonizes the mind, dispels lassitude and relieves fatigue, awakens the thought and prevents drowsiness.

TELL-TALE

The man who comes with a tale about others has himself an axe to grind.

TEMPTATION

Temptation wrings integrity even as the thumbscrew twists a man's fingers.

TENACITY

Tenacity and adversity are old enemies.

THIEVES

Robbers are plundered by thieves.

Thieves in the dark hate the moonlight.

THIRST

Thirst is never quenched by drinking poison.

THOUGHTS

If you wish to know what most occupies a man's thoughts, you have only to listen to his conversation.

As soon as you have made a thought, laugh at it.

Treat thoughts as guests and wishes as children.

Where all thinking is the same, there is very little thinking.

THRIFT

Be thrifty in good times to survive in bad times.

TIGERS

Even a tiger takes a nap from time to time.

The tiger pretends to be a vegetarian.

Do not try to escape a flood by grabbing the tail of a tiger.

Do not shave the head of a tiger with the tail of a snake.

A tiger does not take insults from sheep.

You cannot get a cub unless you go into the tiger's cave.

TIME

Yesterday, today and tomorrow – these are the three days of man.

Yesterday did not stay.

Even the most beautiful morning cannot bring back the evening.

The evening crowns the days.

An inch of time on the sundial is worth more than a foot of jade.

To say, 'I don't have time', is like saying, 'I don't want to'.

To one who waits, a moment seems a year.

With money you can buy a clock but not time.

You can't buy an inch of time with an inch of gold.

Light travels like an arrow, and time like a shuttle.

Time is more important than money.

The most beautiful tomorrow cannot bring yesterday back for us.

TRANSFORMATION

What the caterpillar calls the end, the rest of the world calls a butterfly.

A bar of iron continually ground becomes a needle.

TRANSIENCE

There is no cloth so fine that moths are unable to eat it.

TRAVELLING

He who travels in a splendid carriage, is greeted by strangers as though he were a relative.

Traveller, there is no road. The road is made as you walk.

Only he that has travelled the road knows where the holes are deep.

When you go for a one day trip, carry food for two days.

The traveller's pillow is always cold.

A journey of a thousand miles must begin with a single step.

The journey is the reward.

The carriage wheels are free for a journey to the clouds.

All roads lead to Peking.

If ever you heard people speaking about Peking, then don't go there.

TREASURE

One small grain is the treasure of treasures.

TREES

A tree that can't be spanned by one man, grows from a minuscule seed.

When the tree falls, the shadow flies.

Though a tree be a thousand feet high, the leaves fall and return to the root.

To fell the tree very quickly, you must sharpen the axe twice.

After shaking a tree, shake it again. It costs nothing.

Don't climb a tree to catch a fish.

The best time to plant a tree was 20 years ago. The second best time is today.

He who shakes a tree lightly will get only stupid monkeys.

TROUBLES

Agues come on horseback, but go away on foot.

Blessings do not come in doubles but calamities do.

It is easy to court trouble, but hard to avert it.

Don't trouble trouble until trouble troubles you.

The load carried by another doesn't seem very heavy.

TRUTH

There are different truths: there is my truth, there is your truth and there is the truth.

The truths we like the least are those we should know the best.

Truth is not determined by the volume of the voice.

Some truths can be sensed, but not said.

The pen of the tongue should be dipped in the ink of the heart.

U

UGLINESS

Better to display your ugliness than to hide your ignorance.

Even ugly faces are worth looking at – and that is a great comfort for most people.

UNDERSTANDING

Hear all sides and you will be enlightened. Hear one side, and you will be in the dark.

How can the swallow understand the aspirations of the swan?

The one who understands does not speak; the one who speaks does not understand.

When you cease to strive to understand, then you will know without understanding.

The merchant's daughters do not understand the grief of a lost kingdom.

Reason goes further than the heart, but never far.

UNHAPPINESS

Unhappiness conquers frightened souls, meanwhile great minds tame unhappiness.

Misery acquaints men with strange bedfellows.

UNINTENDED CONSEQUENCES

Throw things at a mouse and you break the vase.

When you aim at the rat, beware of the vase.

Whilst wrangling over a quarter of pig, you can lose a flock of sheep.

The mantis seizes the locust but does not see the yellow bird behind him.

Fighting over a little thing might result in losing everything.

UNITY

With more problems, a nation becomes united.

Unity can turn dirt into gold.

VAINGLORY

Vainglory has flowers but bears no fruit.

VALUE

A picture is worth ten thousand words.

Cheap things are not good, good things are not cheap.

There is no such thing as a worthless person or a tree without roots.

Size is of the least importance, for a giant corpse only feeds more vultures.

Scarcity creates value. Plenty creates complacency.

The sea cannot be measured with a bushel.

VICTORY

To win an argument does not mean you have convinced your opponent.

Victory has a hundred fathers and defeat is an orphan.

Without the fire of enthusiasm there is no warmth in victory.

Supreme excellence consists in breaking the enemy's resistance without fighting.

The weak overcomes the soft and the soft overcomes the hard.

VIOLENCE

The man who strikes first admits that his ideas have given out.

To use violence is to already be defeated.

The one who first resorts to violence shows that he has no more arguments.

VIRTUE

Virtue practised to be seen is not real virtue; vice which fears to be seen is real vice.

The door to virtue is heavy and hard to open.

Good has its reward, and evil has its cost.

Being in the right does not depend on having a loud voice.

WARFARE

Fight poison with poison.

The arrogant army will lose the battle for sure.

Arrogance is the enemy of victory.

A sharp arrow still requires a strong bow.

Use attack as the tactic of defence.

Wait long, strike fast.

A knife does not argue with an axe.

Hear the pig's cries at the butcher's at midnight, and you know what the battlefield is like.

Border guards are food for the wolves and tigers.

Draw the bow but don't shoot – it is a bigger threat to be intimidated than to be hit.

The greatest conqueror wins without struggle.

It is easy to get a thousand soldiers, but difficult to get one general.

The best soldier does not attack.

Nothing brings greater misfortune than killing those who have already surrendered.

All is fair in war.

In times of war there can never be enough trickery.

A weapon is only loyal to the one who uses it.

If one man guards a narrow pass, ten thousand cannot get through.

Swords and guns have no eyes.

Three simple shoemakers equal one brilliant strategist.

Locks can not be made from good iron; soldiers are not made out of good people.

Don't draw a sword against a louse.

WARNINGS

The overturned cart up ahead serves as a warning to the carts behind.

For a villain a warning is just a sigh in the wind.

Kill the chicken to frighten the monkey.

Kill one to warn a hundred.

Give the mule a beating and the horse will also be afraid.

WATER

Water that has reached its level does not flow.

When the water falls the stone becomes visible.

When someone gives you a drop of water reward him with a never-ending source.

The purer the water, the fewer the fish.

Water drowns a good swimmer more often than a bad one.

Water is wine for those in love.

When you drink water, remember where the mountain spring is.

Deep waters flow slowly.

Flowing water doesn't stink, and stinking water doesn't flow.

WAY OF THE WORLD

A wonder lasts but nine days.

Aristocrats dislike people who talk too much.

Distinguished people are apt to be forgetful.

Those who have free seats at the play are the first to hiss.

There is no cure for vulgarity.

For a man who suffers from jaundice, everything is yellow.

The best is often the enemy of the good.

The jail is closed day and night and always full; temples are always open and still empty.

Every drama requires a fool.

All things depart from that which is different from themselves, and follow that which is the same.

From the most ordinary of oysters often come the finest pearls.

Those who wear the silk don't rear the worms.

One man's meat is another man's poison.

Monkey see, monkey do.

Only two gentlemen are very busy in this world: Mister Profit and Mister Glory.

The strongest perfumes attract the ugliest flies.

When a wall is about to collapse, everybody gives it a push.

Even the ten fingers cannot be of equal length.

When you have musk, you will automatically have fragrance.

Long and short match each other.

Candles weep until they are ashes.

You have only just immersed one calabash and another one quickly appears.

In a pool without fish the shrimps are highly praised.

Ivy grows only on walls; porridge sticks only to the pan.

Fat fries and burns itself.

WEAKNESS

If you want to weaken something, make it first very strong.

Overcome one's weaknesses by learning from other's strengths.

Weakness brings life, strength brings death.

WEALTH

You are courting bad luck when you brag about your wealth.

You own many houses and hotels, you only sleep in one bed.

Better to be a free bird on the roof than a wealthy concubine in the house.

If one's aim is wealth one cannot be beneficent; if one's aim is benevolence one cannot be worthy.

A small cottage wherein laughter lives is worth more than a castle full of tears.

When you are dead, your fists are empty.

A craftsman who wants to be rich makes carts and coffins.

When you can put away desire, you're rich indeed.

To pretend to satisfy one's desires with worldly goods is like using straw to put out a fire.

Even though you have ten thousand fields, you can eat but one measure of rice a day.

Those who know when they have enough are rich.

Do not count the things you lost, but the things you still have.

Enough is as good as a feast.

Wealth is but dung, useful only when spread about.

Unjustly got wealth is snow sprinkled with hot water.

Wealth attracts thieves, as beauty attracts evil.

In a country badly governed, wealth is something to be ashamed of.

Wealth comes from hard work; poverty is the result of ill planning.

Much wealth will not come if a little does not go.

One courts misfortune by flaunting wealth.

If you share a man's wealth, try to lessen his misfortune.

When you have wealth, why should you strive for more?

Great wealth implies great loss.

A great fortune depends on luck, a small one on diligence.

Much property is a trap for the stupid.

As long as you have one little hair on your head, you are not bald.

WEALTHY MEN

A wealthy man must fear publicity like a pig that must fear its fatness.

When the wealthy lose weight the poor starve.

Wealthy men have short memories.

When a rich man is involved in a hundred projects, ninety-nine of them make him even richer.

Men mourn for those who leave fortunes behind.

The wealthy add riches to riches; the poor add years to years.

He who is satisfied with himself, is rich.

Those who are prospering do not argue about taxes.

WELLS

It's not that the well is too deep, but rather the rope is too short.

Old wells don't bubble.

If one person builds a well, one thousand families will have water to drink.

The well with the sweetest water is the first to be drained.

WICKEDNESS

To see and listen to the wicked is already the beginning of wickedness.

If your children are wicked they don't deserve to inherit; if they are good and hard working they don't need to.

WILLPOWER

He who can follow his own will is a king.

You can deprive an army of its commander, but you can never deprive a man of his will.

Easier to bend the body than the will.

Great souls have wills; feeble ones have only wishes.

The mind is the lord of man's body.

WIND

If the wind comes from an empty cave, it's not without a reason.

The force of the wind tests the strength of the grass.

A sour wind impales the eyes.

No matter how fiercely the wind may howl, the mountain shall not bow to it.

Light a fire in the face of the wind and you'll burn yourself.

There is no wall through which the wind cannot pass.

Without a head wind a kite cannot fly.

WINE

Nothing in this world can be compared with a glass of wine.

Enjoy the wine you have today and accept the worry when it comes tomorrow.

Droplets of rain can soak through your clothes; goblets of wine can wash away your wealth.

If you don't drink, it doesn't matter what price the wine is.

The wine of your country is always good.

Good wine is the best way to iron out difficulties.

Without wine in the bottle it is hard to have guests.

Three glasses of wine end a hundred quarrels.

WINNINGS

You win by not gambling.

Small winnings make a heavy purse.

WINTER

After a heavy winter comes a sunny spring.

Without the bitter cold of winter, how can one enjoy the fragrance of the plum blossoms?

Better the cold blast of winter than the hot breath of a pursuing elephant.

Heaven doesn't cancel winter because men dislike cold.

WISDOM

A good bee never lands on a fallen flower.

Look within! The secret is inside you.

You need your wits about you the most when you are dealing with an idiot.

The proper man understands equity, the small man profits.

As one lamp serves to dispel a thousand years of darkness, so one flash of wisdom destroys ten thousand years of ignorance.

Wisdom is the best weapon of war.

A wise man is always good but a good man is not always wise.

The beginning of wisdom is to call things by their right names.

Wisdom is attained by learning when to hold one's tongue.

You don't have to go far to find wisdom.

The palace leads to fame; the market to fortune; and loneliness to wisdom.

Of all the stratagems, to know when to quit is the best.

You inherit intelligence, wisdom must be learned.

As the pine and the cedar endure the frost and the snow, so intelligence and wisdom overcome dangers and hardships.

Hear all sides and you will be enlightened. Hear one side, and you will be in the dark.

WISHES

If wishes were horses, beggars would ride.

Our wishes are like little children – the more you indulge them, the more they want from you.

WISHES FOR OTHERS

May it always be spring with you.

May you live in interesting times.

May your life be filled with experiences.

May your way always be enlightened by a lucky star.

May your every wish be granted.

May you come to the attention of those in authority.

May you find what you are looking for.

WOMEN

The woman who tells her age is either too young to have anything to lose or too old to have anything to gain.

A woman can live the life of a prisoner. She can live the life of a princess. Or she can be herself.

When a chaste woman desires pleasure she gets it properly.

Women have long hair but short thoughts.

A woman who sells fans shields her eyes from the sun with her own hands.

Women hold up half the sky.

To tell a secret to a woman is like pricking a soap bubble.

A pretty woman at home is the enemy of all the ugly ones.

A woman's beauty makes fish sink and wild geese fall from the sky.

The first decision of a woman is the most intelligent and the last decision most dangerous.

The tongue of a woman is the sword that is never allowed to rust.

A patient woman can roast an ox with a lantern.

A woman has seven small holes. One of them must not be perfumed.

The mind of a woman is made of mercury, her heart of wax.

One hundred women are not worth a single testicle.

Old women favour six things: pearls, sons-in-law, chickens, future projections, religion and tears.

Woman: young, a goddess; old, a little monkey.

A lazy woman tries to carry everything at the same time.

Pregnant women most of all like bitter food when they are expecting a boy and peppered food when they are expecting a girl.

The advice of a clever woman can ruin a strong town.

The most highly praised woman is the one about whom no one speaks.

The woman with long feet ends up alone in a room.

The woman has seven mouths, and eight languages to chatter in.

A woman with a large tongue is a ladder of misery.

A woman's heart is a needle at the bottom of the sea.

Women never praise without gossiping.

When a woman talks to you, smile but do not listen.

A thriftless woman burns the entire candle looking for a match.

Never does a woman lie in a more cunning way than when she tells the truth to someone who doesn't believe her.

The unfaithful woman has remorse, the faithful one has regret.

A curious woman is capable of turning around the rainbow just to see what is on the other side.

Even a big elephant can be caught in one female hair.

WOOD

Collect a hundred days of wood for one day of fire.

The man who wants wood begins by shaking a tree.

Some people use big pieces of wood to make small articles.

Hard wood and strong bows break easily.

Don't build a new ship out of old wood.

Buy cheap wood and you'll burn your pot.

Straight wood doesn't require the carpenter's tools.

Every kind of wood is grey when it is reduced to ashes.

You cannot make beautiful sculptures from rotten wood.

As long as there are forests, one need not worry about firewood.

WORDS

If one word does not succeed, ten thousand are of no avail.

Bitter words and weak arguments never lead to a solution.

Square words won't fit into a round ear.

Words are empty, but the writing brush leaves traces.

A bad word whispered will echo a hundred miles.

When words lose their meaning, people lose their liberty.

Words without a veil sound brutal.

Bitter words are medicine; sweet words bring illness.

Watch your words and your deeds, for your words shall be spoken and your deeds shall be copied.

Fine words dress ill deeds.

If one word alone is not enough, a thousand words will be wasted.

One good word gives a man more warmth than cotton and silk.

Words that come from the heart stay warm three winters long.

You can live with tea and cold rice but not with cold words.

A word once spoken, an army of chariots cannot overtake it.

WORK

No mill, no meal.

You can't fill your belly painting pictures of bread.

The capable are assigned more tasks.

If you agree to carry the calf, they'll make you carry the cow.

Decisions should not be too clear. Otherwise, when things go wrong you will have to take the blame.

Be first in the field, the last to the couch.

If one man doesn't work the fields, another goes hungry.

A workman must first sharpen his tools if he is to do his work well.

A thousand workers, a thousand plans.

A work ill done must be done twice.

Work and you will be strong; sit and you will stink.

Do your work, then step back.

Pray for what you want, but work for the things you need.

Never was good work done without much trouble.

Choose a job you love, and you will never have to work a day in your life.

Work is afraid of a resolute man.

Even when sandwiches rain from the sky, you will still have to stoop to pick them up.

WORLD AFFAIRS

The world's affairs are but a dream in spring.

The world is doing fine when there is no news to talk about.

The world is our house. Keep it clean.

After all, the world is but a little place.

To know the world's affairs, read historical records.

WORRY

Worry causes ageing.

Worry doesn't seek out people – people find worry on their own.

You may not have long-term worry; there is always short-term crisis.

WRITERS

A good writer does not need a special pen.

He who can handle a writing brush will never have to beg.

WRITING

An obscure style is a blind mirror.

Paper and brush may kill a man; you don't need a knife.

y

YIN AND YANG

Yin and Yang unify the hearts.

YOUTH

A youth is to be regarded with respect.

How do you know that a youth's future will not be equal to our present?

When youth takes the scorpion for a bed-fellow, the aged go out on the roof.

Inferior in youth, not much use in old age.

His mouth still smells of mother's milk.

A young branch takes on all the bends that one gives it.

You are not as young as you were but nowhere near as old as you hope to become.

It's always young men that can enjoy the love of a goddess.

The Yangtse never runs backwards; man recaptures not his youth.